21 Days
Of Intentional Prayer

A Workbook of Guided Prayers to Help You Reflect and Reset

twenty somethin & black

Day 1
Setting Your Intention

Dear Lord,

I'm claiming {INSERT WHAT YOU'RE CLAIMING} for my life. I pray that you give me the deference to know when something, or someone, is pulling me closer to or pushing me further away from my intention. Direct me on the correct path to alleviate myself from any influence that will hinder my progress.

Lord, give me the guidance and conviction I need to achieve what is on my heart.

In your name, Amen.

Affirmation of the Day: I claim that this next year will be great and prosperity will be mine.

Day 1
Space to Reflect

Day 2
Financial Growth

Dear Lord,

I pray this year brings me financial wealth and supernatural increase beyond what I think is possible. Lord, I pray for the ability to provide for myself financially and afford everything I need to prosper in life.

Give me the faith to know that you will always provide for me despite what I see in my bank account.

Protect my finances and give me the financial wisdom to identify what I want versus what I need, so that my financial goals can come into fruition.

In your name, Amen.

Affirmation of the Day: I welcome an unlimited source of income and wealth in my life with the necessary knowledge and wisdom to properly be a good financial steward.

Day 2
Space to Reflect

twenty *somethin'* & *black*

Day 3
New Experiences

Dear Lord,

Give me the courage to go outside of my comfort zone. Reveal to me the beauty in saying "yes" to experiences that I typically would say "no" to out of fear or stubbornness.

Allow me to welcome new opportunities into my life. Show me the rewards of doors opening when I become receptive to new things. Guide me in the embracing of change in all its beautiful forms.

In your name, Amen.

Affirmation of the Day: I am open to new experiences, I am open to new ways of doing things in order to broaden my horizon and influence in my purpose.

Day 3
Space to Reflect

twenty somethin' & black

Day 4

Mental Health

Dear Lord,

Protect and preserve my mind, body, and spirit. Allow me to see the beauty in treating my body and mind as the gift that you have created it to be.

Father, don't let me fall for the temptation of habits, thought processes, and foods that aren't beneficial to my growth. Keep me motivated to workout regularly. Keep me motivated to think positively. Keep me motivated to uplift myself and others around me.

Don't let me take my youth for granted.

In your name, Amen.

Affirmation of the Day: I love myself for who I am, as I am.

Day 4
Space to Reflect

_____

_____

_____

_____

_____

_____

_____

_____

_____

Day 5

Career

Dear Lord,

You've placed me on this Earth for a purpose. Align my career and side hustle(s) with the purpose you've assigned to me before I even knew my own name.

Give me success, but more importantly, give me guidance to know when I am, and am not, operating in my purpose. Grant me the discernment to know that if something is for me, it is for me no matter what…especially when it comes to my career and side hustles.

Protect me from the turmoil that setbacks can bring. Instead, help me find motivation in the setbacks and use them as fuel to keep me moving forward in my aspirations.

I pray I see success in my career and side hustles.

In your name, Amen.

Affirmation of the Day: Today I will make time to work on personal goals that are important to me, in order to devise a clear plan of action.

Day 5
Space to Reflect

Day 6
Healing from Bad Relationships

Dear Lord,

Everyone isn't for me and that's okay. Help me to forgive those who hurt me in the past, in order to heal. Thank you for the revelation that even those who hurt me are apart of my story to strengthen me.

Fill me with the needed grace to extend to forgive those who have done me wrong and heal from that pain. Give me the courage to open myself up to people who love and appreciate me.

Allow me to let go of guilt and bitterness that I have towards those situations and people, so that I can welcome the love you've intended for me to receive and experience.

Father, help me be transparent with you whenever I get caught up in those hurtful situations so that we can navigate through it together. You have someone perfect for me in store. Help me to make room in my life for them, by laying all the past pain and disappointment at your feet.

In your name, Amen.

Affirmation of the Day: I forgive those who have done me wrong, and let go of any negative thoughts towards others in the past to prepare for my future success.

Day 6
Space to Reflect

twenty *somethin'* & *black*

Day 7
Debt-Free Mindset

Lord,

Put me in a debt-free state of mind. You didn't intend for me to live in debt, therefore I do not accept a lifestyle of debt. Help me to stay motivated to erase all the debt I'm currently carrying. Keep me motivated to live as you intended, owing nothing to anyone.

Most importantly, help me understand that this is a journey, not an overnight trip. It took time to acquire the debt and will take time to get rid of it. Give me the patience to trust the process.

Give me guidance to know what the necessary steps are to be debt-free and live a financially responsible life.

In your name, Amen.

Affirmation of the Day: I will make the necessary changes to be debt-free and continue to make the right financial choices to support a lifestyle without debt.

Day 7
Space to Reflect

Day 8

Trust the Process

Dear Lord,

Life is all about the journey, right? So, help me appreciate the process. Help me appreciate the lows of my growth just as much as the highs because they all work together to serve a purpose.

Help me to enjoy the current season of my life that I am in right now, even if it's not where I thought that I would be.

In your name, Amen.

Affirmation of the Day: I trust the process and everything life brings on my journey to fulfilling my purpose.

Day 8
Space to Reflect

Day 9
Saying Goodbye to Unwanted Habits

Dear Lord,

Anything that is not of You that is within me, please get rid of it. I don't want to have habits that are not beneficial in my walk with you anymore.

Show me my flaws, so that I can correct them. Show me my bad habits, so that I can work through the inferior mindset that entices me to engage in that behavior to make myself better.

In your name, Amen.

Affirmation of the Day: I let go of things in my life that are blocking my growth.

Day 9
Space to Reflect

Day 10
Accomplish Career Goals

Dear Lord,

Help me to be the best professional that I can be. Remind me that I am working not for the praise of others, but rather, to be a beacon of light representing all of God's promises fulfilled. Help me to remain consistent with excellent work ethic, values, and practices. Show me how to put forth my very best in all things that I do.

Do not let me procrastinate or let things fall to the wayside. Keep me on point in every aspect of my life so that I can achieve any career goals that I set my mind to accomplish.

In your name, Amen.

Affirmation of the Day: I can accomplish all of my career goals. I will be successful in all that I do.

Day 10
Space to Reflect

Day 11
Finding Love Within Myself

Dear Lord,

I am perfectly made by You. Just like you constructed every part of Adam and Eve, remind me that you have also constructed me perfectly in your image. From each hair on my head, to the toes on my feet – I am beautifully and wonderfully made.

Don't let me forget that revelation by listening to the world's standards of beauty. Give me the confidence to appreciate how you've made me flaws and all.

In your name, Amen.

Affirmation of the Day: I love myself, and fully appreciate my flaws and strengths equally because they work together to make me who I am.

Day 11

Space to Reflect

twenty *somethin'* & *black*

Day 12

Strengthen my Relationship with God

Dear Lord,

I want you in my life to guide me and cultivate me into the person that I'm called to be. I cast out any guilt or shame that I may have due to deviation from Your path in the past. Lord I need you and your direction. I want to feel your presence with me all day, every day.

Be at the center of my life and in everything I do. Take the wheel Lord, I trust you.

In your name, Amen.

Affirmation of the Day: I love myself, and fully appreciate my flaws and strengths equally because they work together to make me who I am.

Day 12
Space to Reflect

Day 13

Strengthen my Relationship with God

Dear Lord,

I want you in my life to guide me and cultivate me into the person that I'm called to be. I cast out any guilt or shame that I may have from any deviation from Your path in the past. Lord I need you and your direction. I want to feel your presence with me all day, every day.

Be at the center of my life and in everything I do. Take the wheel Lord, I trust you.

In your name, Amen.

Affirmation of the Day: I love myself, and fully appreciate my flaws and strengths equally because they work together to make me who I am.

Day 13
Space to Reflect

_____

_____

_____

_____

_____

_____

_____

_____

_____

Day 14

Strengthen my Relationship with God

Dear Lord,

Even though there are moments when I get frustrated that I can't afford everything I want, allow me to appreciate that I'm able to afford everything that I need. Give me the positive perspective to appreciate all that I have as a blessing.

I have the resources Lord, but admittedly sometimes I misuse them. Teach me how to make the most out of my current financial situation.

In your name, Amen.

Affirmation of the Day: Give me the gratitude with my current finances that I have been trusted with to prepare for increased financial blessings.

Day 14
Space to Reflect

Day 15

Treating my Body Right and Internalize Knowing my Body is a Temple

Dear Lord,

Allow me to see my body in the same way that you have since my creation, as a beautiful masterpiece.

My body is my temple. I pray that I am always reminded of that and desire to take care of it. Show me how to properly care for my temple.

In your name, Amen.

Affirmation of the Day: I will treat my body with respect because it's a direct representation of God's love for me.

Day 15
Space to Reflect

Day 16

Career and Entrepreneurial Motivation

Dear Lord,

Give me the focus and energy to prioritize my time efficiently and effectively, so that I can accomplish everything you've called me to do.

Motivate me, Lord. Strengthen me in times of weakness and fatigue so that I can still have the drive to get things done.

I know that you have big plans for me. Give me the clarity and tenacity to see those plans through.

In your name, Amen.

Affirmation of the Day: I have the vision and energy to focus all my efforts on the things I want to accomplish in life to be successful.

Day 16
Space to Reflect

_____

_____

_____

_____

_____

_____

_____

_____

_____

_____

twenty somethin' & black

Day 17

Break Free from all Toxic Habits in my Relationships with Others

Dear Lord,

Remove anything and anyone in my life that isn't good for me. Give me the strength to accept that I'm not meant for everyone and everyone isn't meant for me.

Give me insight into the roles that I play in my relationships and correct anything within me that may be harmful to others.

In your name, Amen.

Affirmation of the Day: I abandon old habits and choose new, positive ones to uplift myself and others.

Day 17
Space to Reflect

Day 18

Being a Strong Person

Dear Lord,

Allow me to see my own strength and abilities despite any negativity from external sources.

Elevate me to develop those gifts that you have placed within me to make an impact. Give me the courage to not dim my light or dumb down my greatness to make others comfortable. If someone cannot handle me in my strength, remove them from my life.

In your name, Amen.

Affirmation of the Day: I am strong. I have the courage and inner peace necessary to thrive in greatness.

Day 18
Space to Reflect

Day 19

God Guides me in Everything I Do

Dear Lord,

Give me the courage to trust you with EVERYTHING. Allow me to let go of wanting to have control.

There have been moments in the past, when I made my own decisions and ended up back in the same situation. I know you have more planned for me Lord, but I am too comfortable with this cycle of limited progress.

Place on my heart discomfort with staying in this same position so that I may grow. I trust that you only want what is best for me. I trust you, fully.

Guide me, Lord.

In your name, Amen.

Affirmation of the Day: I give you all of me, Lord. Everything that I do, cannot be successful without You.

Day 19
Space to Reflect

_____

_____

_____

_____

_____

_____

_____

_____

_____

Day 20

I am Open to Love.

Dear Lord,

When it comes to my next/current relationship, I want what you want for me. Cultivate a mutual attraction between the right person and I. Bring forth a person that will be beneficial to my life and align with the person that I want to be currently and in the future. Match me someone who is equally yoked with me.

In your name, Amen.

Affirmation of the Day: I am open to new relationships, new experiences, and letting love in.

Day 20

Space to Reflect

Day 21

Prayer Changes Things

Dear Lord,

Allow me to trust the power of prayer. Train me to go to you in prayer before I seek advice from the world or rely solely on my own understanding.

Give me the patience and trust required to allow you to guide everything I do. Open my ears and my heart to hear you clearly when I pray.

In your name, Amen.

Affirmation of the Day: I know that prayer has the power to change any and every thing that has a hold on my life. I submit myself to You in prayer and trust You with me.

Day 21
Space to Reflect

About Twenty Somethin' & Black

Twenty Somethin' & Black was manifested from the belief that young women can learn how to navigate various areas of life through God, community and 'good ol' girl talk'. Created with the young professional and recent college graduate in mind, our content focuses on helping women "get it together" when it comes to advancing their career, improving finances, fostering relationships, prioritizing health and unapologetically exploring faith.

Devotional Created By: Derika Crowley (Twenty Somethin' & Black Co-Founder)
Edited by: Brianna Forde (Twenty Somethin' & Black Co-Founder) and Brianna Elmore (Twenty Somethin' & Black Editor-In-Chief)

Extra Space to Write

Extra Space to Write

Extra Space to Write

Extra Space to Write

twenty *somethin'* & *black*

www.ingramcontent.com/pod-product-compliance
Lightning Source LLC
Chambersburg PA
CBHW032137090426
42743CB00007B/620